Let Go & Choose You!

A Meditation Journal for Self-Affirmation

This journal encourages you to let go of what doesn't enhance your life and choose what does. Each thought-provoking question is designed to help you examine the various aspects of your situation from a broad perspective. Affirming your self-worth with positive "I AM" statements will boost your confidence to be who you're meant to be – strong, smart, beautiful, and courageous. Using this journal every day will help you cast off the trivial aspects that bog you down and instead cherish the vital ones that make your life shine.

Thank You

Queen Renae!

Lakeesha Jones

Let Go & Choose You!

ℰ

Lakeesha Jones

ℰ

Published by

Grand Rising Press

Minneapolis, Minnesota

Cover design by Patience Epps

ISBN: 979-8-9895361-0-8

First Addition: December, 2023

Printed in the United States of America

LET GO & CHOOSE YOU!

Table of Contents

Author's Introduction - I got this!

Letting go of what holds you back, and choosing what sets you free takes time and commitment. But I've discovered, as you will, how powerfully freeing it feels. In my own life, I've endured too many trials and tribulations to count. But those troubled times have taught me some very practical lessons. I've created this working journal to share what I've learned with you.

Letting Go and Choosing Me may sound selfish, but I've discovered that taking care of "me first" is actually the best way to take care of those around me. Because only if I am healthy and content in my own life can I offer reliable support to others.

This journal will help you understand your own inner strength, and how to use it. When times get rough, you'll pause to reflect, to be gentle with yourself, to write out your thoughts, and talk with others when you need to. Then you'll choose what's truly best for you. Just as I did, you'll put one foot in front of the other and walk, then run, then fly like the wind!

Remember, it's okay to mess up at times. We all do. But even when you do, your feelings and needs still deserve respect. You'll always allow yourself to feel what you feel, to sit in it for a while without judging yourself. Then you'll work through your feelings using self-reflection, journal writing, and talking things out, in order to understand where these feelings come from and what your real needs are.

LET GO & CHOOSE YOU!

The journey can be grueling if you try to go at it alone. Comforting friends will make all the difference. So you'll gather with like-minded individuals whose love and positivity will support you. Their encouragement will see you through difficult times and inspire you to reach your goals. And you will do the same for them!

By using this journal, you'll gain valuable tools to aid your self-reflection, beginning with a daily practice of self-affirmation, then adding daily meditation guided by thought-provoking questions. You'll also feel the relaxing benefits of keeping a personal journal, where you can open up and be completely honest. Since no one but you will see it, you can explore your fears, weaknesses, and vulnerabilities in complete privacy. You'll make lists of your goals, both small and huge, and you'll set your priorities, putting the most essential things first. Eventually, you'll find how grounding this process can be, by clearing your mind and centering you.

Choosing You means giving yourself time to do the work you need. So let's get started now!

Statements of Self-Affirmation

A daily practice of self-affirmation takes only two minutes each morning. First, face yourself in the mirror and smile. Then make a positive statement about yourself. Repeat it 10 times, slowly, allowing yourself to absorb the full meaning of your words. The list below will help you begin. Just choose what means the most to you and say it to yourself. In time, this practice will boost you self-confidence and improve your state of mind. It sounds simple, but believe me, it works!

I am Active	I am Energized
I am Adaptable	I am Faithful
I am Authentic	I am Friendly
I am Beautiful	I am Funny
I am Brave	I am Generous
I am Brilliant	I am Grateful
I am Capable	I am Growing
I am Caring	I am Hardworking
I am Creative	I am Helpful
I am Daring	I am Honest
I am Decisive	I am Inclusive
I am Dependable	I am Inspiring
I am Encouraging	I am Intelligent
I am Empathetic	I am Jazzy

LET GO & CHOOSE YOU!

I am Joyful

I am Just

I am Kid-Friendly

I am Kind

I am Knowledgeable

I am Likable

I am Learning

I am Loyal

I am Magical

I am Merciful

I am Motivated

I am Open-minded

I am Optimistic

I am Outstanding

I am Patient

I am Peaceful

I am Powerful

I am Qualified

I am Quick-witted

I am Questioning

I am Radiant

I am Reliable

I am Respected

I am Self-confident

I am Sincere

I am Strong

I am Talented

I am Tolerant

I am Trustworthy

I am Unique

I am Unstoppable

I am Useful

I am Valuable

I am Venturesome

I am Versatile

I am Warmhearted

I am Wise

I am Whole

I am eXotic

I am Yearning

I am Young-at-heart

I am Zesty

Daily Meditation with Chakras

The ancient Chakra, or wheel, symbolizes the seven major energy centers of the human body, each of which has a specific color, action, purpose, and mantra statement. Chakra mediation not only relieves stress and helps you relax, it also guides you to explore your feelings, needs and life goals. To begin, sit in a quiet comfortable place and allow yourself to just breath for a minute or two. Then move through each Chakra, starting with the Root. Read its action, purpose, and mantra statement. Then think quietly about how it applies to your life. In the journal pages which follow, you'll find probing questions to guide your meditation and writing.

Root: Grounding

Action – to be centered

Purpose – to feel comfortable in my own skin

Mantra – By keeping my body healthy, I will feel secure about myself and my abilities.

Sacral: Relationships

Action – to feel

Purpose – to connect emotionally with other people and ideas

Mantra – Healthy relationships and sexuality will make me happier and more creative.

Solar Plexus: Power

Action – to take action

Purpose – to use the power within you

Mantra – By knowing and activating my power, I will accomplish my life's purpose.

Heart: Compassion

Action – to love

Purpose – to feel compassion for yourself and others

Mantra – Loving myself and others will lead me to deeper human understanding.

Throat: Expression

Action – to speak

Purpose – to freely express your ideas and feelings

Mantra – Speaking up will add my truth to the human conversation.

Third Eye: Insight

Action – to see

Purpose – to strengthen your inner sight

Mantra – Trusting my intuition and imagination will broaden my horizons.

Crown: Spirituality

Action – to know

Purpose – to explore the spiritual meaning of life

Mantra – Knowing my purpose in life will bring inner peace.

LET GO & CHOOSE YOU!

Root: Grounding

Action: to be centered
Purpose: to feel comfortable in my own skin
Mantra: by keeping my body healthy, I will feel secure about myself and abilities

What does being grounded mean to me?

Let Go: Do I feel stable, sensible, and steady, with my feet firmly on the ground?

What does being grounded mean to me?

Choose You: How can I benefit from feeling more grounded in my life?

Am I a stable person?

Let Go: Are there times when I feel out of control? If so, when?

Am I a stable person?

Choose You: How will I get help to feel more centered and in control?

Am I meeting my basic needs?

Let Go: Do I feel safe, healthy, and comfortable in my surroundings? If not, why?

Am I meeting my basic needs?

Choose You: How can I meet my basic needs more successfully?

Do I use good sense when making decisions?

Let Go: Have I ever done things that go against good sense?

Do I use good sense when making decisions?

Choose You: Next time I feel tempted to ignore good sense, how will I make a better choice?

How well do I take care of my personal needs?

Let Go: What self-care do I use on a daily basis? Is it enough?

How well do I take care of my personal needs?

Choose You: What are some things I can do to treat myself better?

Do I ever feel that I'm just drifting through life?

Let Go: What direction is my life taking, and do I like it?

Do I ever feel that I'm just drifting through life?

Choose You: How can I steer a happier course through life?

Am I ever my own worst enemy?

Let Go: Have I ever engaged in self-sabotaging behavior?

Am I ever my own worst enemy?

Choose You: What will I do to choose self-affirmation instead?

How well do I deal with stress?

Let Go: What kind of stress am I dealing with? What causes it?

How well do I deal with stress?

Choose You: What tools can I use to manage stress better, and how will this benefit me?

When my energy feels drained, how can restore it?

Let Go: What is draining my energy, whether physical, mental or spiritual?

When my energy feels drained, how can restore it?

Choose You: How can I have more energy and use it more wisely?

How can friendship, love, and support help me feel grounded?

Let Go: How do my friends or partner help me feel more stable and steady?

How can friendship, love, and support help me feel grounded?

Choose You: If I'm not getting the support I need, how can I find it?

NOW, WRITE FREELY ABOUT YOUR EXPERIENCES WITH FEELING GROUNDED.

LET GO & CHOOSE YOU!

Sacral: Relationships

Action: to feel
Purpose: to connect emotionally with other people and ideas
Mantra: Healthy relationships and sexuality will make me happier and more creative

What do I want most from a relationship right now?

Let Go: What needs do I have that a relationship might fill?

What do I want most from a relationship right now?

Choose You: What do I want to give and receive in my current or future relationship?

Do I have a friend with whom I can completely open up about my feelings?

Let Go: What are my experiences with friendships?

Do I have a friend with whom I can completely open up about my feelings?

Choose You: What friend can I call in the middle of the night if I just need to talk?

Am I ready for a long-term committed relationship?

Let Go: What are my experiences with long-term relationships?

Am I ready for a long-term committed relationship?

Choose You: Why do I want, or not want, a long-term committed relationship?

Do I believe that a loyal relationship will make me happier and healthier?

Let Go: What are my experiences with loyalty?

Do I believe that a loyal relationship will make me happier and healthier?

Choose You: What does a loyal relationship look like to me, and what are the benefits?

Can I still be myself while feeling connected in a relationship?

Let Go: Do I currently have a strong sense of my own individuality? Why or why not?

Can I still be myself while feeling connected in a relationship?

Choose You: What can I do today to strengthen and maintain my own sense of self?

Am I secure enough to wait for the right person, or will I settle for less?

Let Go: In my past experience, have I ever settled for less? Why or why not?

Am I secure enough to wait for the right person, or will I settle for less?

Choose You: What characteristics am I looking for in my ideal partner?

Am I holding onto my anger, and is it helping or hurting me?

Let Go: What are some things I feel angry about in a current or past relationship?

LET GO & CHOOSE YOU!

Am I holding onto my anger, and is it helping or hurting me?

Choose You: What can I do to release this anger and move past it?

What changes must I make to adapt to a new relationship?

Let Go: What are my experiences with compromise in a new relationship?

What changes must I make to adapt to a new relationship?

Choose You: What can I do to make a normal period of adjustment easier?

Do I honestly admire my friends and partner?

Let Go: What do I admire about the people I care about?

Do I honestly admire my friends and partner?

Choose You: If I don't honestly admire a friend/partner, what will I do?

Are my friends/partner and I honest with each other?

Let Go: How can I be more honest in my relationships?

LET GO & CHOOSE YOU!

Are my friends/partner and I honest with each other?

Choose You: How can I make it easier for my friends/partner to be honest with me?

Now, write freely about your relationships.

LET GO & CHOOSE YOU!

Solar Plexus: Power

Action: to take action
Purpose: to use the power within you
Mantra: By knowing and activating my power, I will accomplish my life's purpose

What makes me feel strong?

Let Go: Am I as physically, mentally and spiritually strong as I want to be? Why or why not?

What makes me feel strong?

Choose You: What's holding me back from feeling stronger?

Do I understand the many types of power?

Let Go: What does power look like to me? Where does it come from?

Do I understand the many types of power?

Choose You: How do my intelligence, skills, work, friendship, and ethics give me power?

What power do I have to control my own life?

Let Go: Do I really use the power I have? Why or why not?

LET GO & CHOOSE YOU!

What power do I have to control my own life?

Choose You: How can I use my power more effectively to control my life?

What power do I have to make the world better?

Let Go: If I had the power to make a real impact in the world, what would I do?

LET GO & CHOOSE YOU!

What power do I have to make the world better?

Choose You: How can I accept that I do already have that power?

How will I use my power?

Let Go: Will I use my power for myself, or for others, or both?

How will I use my power?

Choose You: What are the many ways in which I can use my power for good?

How does the color of my skin affect my power?

Let Go: What are my experiences with my skin color?

How does the color of my skin affect my power?

Choose You: How can I believe more deeply in the beauty of my skin color?

How does my appearance affect my power?

Let Go: What is my experience with my appearance?

How does my appearance affect my power?

Choose you: How can I enhance my unique appearance to feel more powerful?

Will my current health habits keep me strong?

Let Go: How well do I take care of my health?

Will my current health habits keep me strong?

Choose You: What health habits can I add for a stronger mind, body, and spirit?

Am I ignoring my pain in an attempt to be strong?

Let Go: Have I ever used strength to hide pain? Did it help?

LET GO & CHOOSE YOU!

Am I ignoring my pain in an attempt to be strong?

Choose You: Why do I feel the need to hide pain, and what will I do about it?

Do I truly believe I hold the power to heal myself?

Let Go: What deep wounds do I have that need healing?

Do I truly believe I hold the power to heal myself?

Choose You: What powerful steps can I take to begin my healing journey?

NOW WRITE FREELY ABOUT THE POWER YOU HAVE TO HELP YOURSELF AND THOSE AROUND YOU.

LET GO & CHOOSE YOU!

Heart: Compassion

Action: to love
Purpose: to feel compassion for yourself and others
Mantra: loving myself and others will lead me to deeper human understanding

Who in my life do I truly love, and how do I show it?

Let Go: How do I define love – as a feeling, or an action?

Who in my life do I truly love, and how do I show it?

Choose You: What actions can I take to show my love more fully?

Who truly loves me, and how do they show it?

Let Go: What are my experiences with allowing others to love and believe in me?

Who truly loves me, and how do they show it?

Choose You: How can I be more open to love?

Do I truly know how to empathize and show kindness?

Let Go: What do empathy and kindness mean to me?

Do I truly know how to empathize and show kindness?

Choose You: How can I get better at empathizing and showing kindness to others?

Do I know how to say, "I'm sorry?"

Let Go: Have I ever hurt someone, then failed to apologize?

LET GO & CHOOSE YOU!

Do I know how to say, "I'm sorry?"

Choose You: How can an honest apology help me as much as the other person?

Can I find it in my heart to forgive?

Let Go: What is my experience with forgiving people when they hurt me?

LET GO & CHOOSE YOU!

Can I find it in my heart to forgive?

Choose You: How can I get better at offering forgiveness?

How can I show compassion to myself?

Let Go: Do I genuinely love myself? Why or why not?

How can I show compassion to myself?

Choose You: How can I forgive my mistakes and show myself more kindness?

Do I believe that I am worthy of respect?

Let Go: What are my experiences with self-respect and respect from others?

Do I believe that I am worthy of respect?

Choose You: How can I remind myself that I am worthy of respect?

Can I accept well-meant criticism without feeling offended?

Let Go: What are my past experiences with receiving criticism?

Can I accept well-meant criticism without feeling offended?

Choose You: How can I be more open to criticism and put it to better use?

How do I feel about unconditional love?

Let Go: What is my experience with unconditional love, both positive and negative?

How do I feel about unconditional love?

Choose You: Who should have my unconditional love, and how will I show it?

Do I have a healthy balance of love?

Let Go: Do I feel the love I give and the love I receive are in balance? Why or why not?

Do I have a healthy balance of love?

Choose You: How can I create a healthier balance of love in my life?

Now, write freely about compassion, kindness, forgiveness, and love.

Throat: Expression

Action: to speak
Purpose: to freely express your ideas and feelings
Mantra: speaking up will add my truth to the human conversation

Why does my voice matter?

Let Go: Do I feel it's important for my voice to be heard? Why or why not?

Why does my voice matter?

Choose You: What are some of the things that I have a lot to say about?

What can I do to be more effective when I speak?

Let Go: Do I feel confident and persuasive when I speak? Why or why not?

What can I do to be more effective when I speak?

Choose You: What can I do to feel more confident and persuasive?

Do I sometimes hold back from speaking my truth?

Let Go: If I've ever held back from speaking my truth, what was the reason?

Do I sometimes hold back from speaking my truth?

Choose You: Should I always speak the truth no matter the situation? Why or why not?

How has my past affected my willingness to speak up?

Let Go: What experiences of speaking up have not gone well for me?

How has my past affected my willingness to speak up?

Choose You: What have I learned that will help me next time?

Do I sometimes force myself to be someone I'm not?

Let Go: Have I ever felt the need to say something I don't mean, and if so, why?

Do I sometimes force myself to be someone I'm not?

Choose You: What steps can I take to be more truly myself when I speak?

What does authenticity mean to me?

Let Go: How do I define being authentic?

What does authenticity mean to me?

Choose You: If I want to be more authentic, what is one step I can take today?

Can positive self-talk help me be more myself?

Let Go: Do I sometimes lose sight of my strengths, talents, and good qualities?

Can positive self-talk help me be more myself?

Choose You: How can I use positive self-talk in my daily routine to help me remember?

When others speak, how well do I listen?

Let Go: Am I good listener, or do I interrupt, offer advice, or turn the conversation to myself?

When others speak, how well do I listen?

Choose You: How can you really pay attention to understand what someone else says?

How should I respond to negative speech?

Let Go: Do I believe that negative speech causes harm? Why or why not?

LET GO & CHOOSE YOU!

How should I respond to negative speech?

Choose You: How should I respond to negative speech in a positive way?

Do I speak up when I need help?

Let Go: Do I currently struggle to ask for help? Why or why not?

Do I speak up when I need help?

Choose You: How can I feel more confident about asking for help when I need it?

Now, write freely about how well you express yourself.

LET GO & CHOOSE YOU!

Third Eye: Insight

Action: to see
Purpose: to strengthen your inner sight
Mantra: trusting my intuition and imagination will broaden my horizons

How can I achieve more meaningful insights?

Let Go: In what areas of my life do I need greater insight?

LET GO & CHOOSE YOU!

How can I achieve more meaningful insights?

Choose You: How can I be open to my own insights when they come?

How much do I trust my own intuition?

Let Go: When I have an insight, does it feel true?

How much do I trust my own intuition?

Choose You: Should I let my insights guide my actions? Why or why not?

In what area of my life do I need inspiration right now?

Let Go: Do I feel that I lack inspiration? Why or why not?

LET GO & CHOOSE YOU!

In what area of my life do I need inspiration right now?

Choose You: In the past, where have my inspirations come from?

What insights do I have about the challenges or obstacles I'm facing now?

Let Go: What challenges or obstacles am I currently facing now?

What insights do I have about the challenges or obstacles I'm facing now?

Choose You: What does insight tell me about my challenges or obstacles?

How can I recognize my own personal goals?

Let Go: What are my dreams and my talents, and how can I fit them together?

How can I recognize my own personal goals?

Choose You: What do my insights tell me about what I can achieve?

Will a vision board help me see my future more clearly?

Let Go: What future do I really want for myself?

LET GO & CHOOSE YOU!

Will a vision board help me see my future more clearly?

Choose You: What items will I place on my vision board to symbolize that future?

Where do I see myself in three to five years?

Let Go: Where do I see my career, relationships, and health in three to five years?

Where do I see myself in three to five years?

Choose You: What three things can I do to move closer to where I want to be?

What does my intuition tell me about hope?

Let Go: What do I hope for, and is my hope useful?

LET GO & CHOOSE YOU!

What does my intuition tell me about hope?

Choose You: How will keeping hope help me survive setbacks?

How can insights help me stay motivated?

Let Go: How truly motivated to achieve my goals do I feel right now?

How can insights help me stay motivated?

Choose You: How can I get motivated to turn insights into action toward my goals?

Will freeing my imagination help me be more creative?

Let Go: How do I feel about my own imagination and creativity?

Will freeing my imagination help me be more creative?

Choose You: How will I use my imagination this week to do something creative?

Now make a list of your goals and put them in priority order.

LET GO & CHOOSE YOU!

Crown: Spiritulity

Action: to know
Purpose: to explore the spiritual meaning of life
Mantra: knowing my purpose in life will bring inner peace

What are my thoughts about a higher power?

Let Go: What do I currently believe about a higher power?

What are my thoughts about a higher power?

Choose You: Whatever my belief, how can I explore my spirituality to achieve balance?

Did I have any past spiritual experiences that affect my attitude today?

Let Go: What positive and/or negative spiritual experiences have I had?

Did I have any past spiritual experiences that affect my attitude today?

Choose You: How am I going to use those experiences in my spiritual journey?

How can I remain peaceful and focused when the world is chaotic?

Let Go: How do current world events make me feel?

How can I remain peaceful and focused when the world is chaotic?

Choose You: How can spirituality help me feel more peaceful and focused?

Will a regular spiritual practice make me more content?

Let Go: What spiritual practices have I tried in the past, and did they help?

Will a regular spiritual practice make me more content?

Choose You: What spiritual practice most appeals to me, and why?

How can a sense of gratitude strengthen my spirit?

Let Go: When in my life have, I've felt grateful, and how did it make me feel?

How can a sense of gratitude strengthen my spirit?

Choose You: How can I feel gratitude on a daily basis?

Can I use this moment now to count my blessings?

Let Go: What are some blessings in my life which I take for granted?

LET GO & CHOOSE YOU!

Can I use this moment now to count my blessings?

Choose You: How can counting my blessings make me a happier person?

Can a healthier spirit help me break unhealthy habits or thinking patterns?

Let Go: What unhealthy habits and thinking patterns have I fallen into, and why?

Can a healthier spirit help me break unhealthy habits or thinking patterns?

Choose You: What is holding me back from achieving spiritual health?

How can a healthy spirit help me adapt to change in my life?

Let Go: What is my experience with change? Am I open to change?

LET GO & CHOOSE YOU!

How can a healthy spirit help me adapt to change in my life?

Choose You: How can I learn to accept that change is necessary?

How will a healthy spirit help me deal with fear?

Let Go: Why am I fearful of stepping out of my comfort zone?

LET GO & CHOOSE YOU!

How will a healthy spirit help me deal with fear?

Choose You: How will stepping out of my comfort zone help me grow?

How will I add a moment of spiritual peace to my schedule today?

Let Go: Do I usually experience spiritual peace in my schedule?

LET GO & CHOOSE YOU!

How will I add a moment of spiritual peace to my schedule today?

Choose You: What will a moment of spiritual peace do for my energy level?

Now, write freely about how your spiritual feelings affect you.

LET GO & CHOOSE YOU!

My Chakra Pledge to Myself

I have decided to Let Go & Chose Me in order to become the best version of myself. I will continue using Chakra Meditation to reflect on the state of my body, mind, and spirit, and I will affirm my strengths through positive self-talk and self-care. I will respect and love myself and those close to me. I will surround myself with positive individuals who inspire me. I will listen, forgive, be kind, and feel grateful. I AM happy and grateful for being ME!